POETRY FROM CRESCENT MOON

William Shakespeare: *The Sonnets*
edited, with an introduction by Mark Tuley

William Shakespeare: *Complete Poems*
edited and introduced by Mark Tuley

Shakespeare: Love, Poetry and Magic in Shakespeare's Sonnets and Plays
by B.D. Barnacle

Elizabethan Sonnet Cycles
edited and introduced by Mark Tuley

Edmund Spenser: *Heavenly Love: Selected Poems*
selected and introduced by Teresa Page

Edmund Spenser: *Amoretti*
edited by Teresa Page

Robert Herrick: *Delight In Disorder: Selected Poems*
edited and introduced by M.K. Pace

Sir Thomas Wyatt: *Love For Love: Selected Poems*
selected and introduced by Louise Cooper

John Donne: *Air and Angels: Selected Poems*
selected and introduced by A.H. Ninham

D.H. Lawrence: *Being Alive: Selected Poems*
edited with an introduction by Margaret Elvy

D.H. Lawrence: Symbolic Landscapes
by Jane Foster

D.H. Lawrence: Infinite Sensual Violence
by M.K. Pace

Percy Bysshe Shelley: *Paradise of Golden Lights: Selected Poems*
selected and introduced by Charlotte Greene

Thomas Hardy: *Her Haunting Ground: Selected Poems*
edited, with an introduction by A.H. Ninham

Sexing Hardy: Thomas Hardy and Feminism
by Margaret Elvy

Emily Bronte: *Darkness and Glory: Selected Poems*
selected and introduced by Miriam Chalk

John Keats: *Bright Star: Selected Poems*
edited with an introduction by Miriam Chalk

John Keats: *Poems of 1820*
edited with an introduction by Miriam Chalk

Henry Vaughan: *A Great Ring of Pure and Endless Light: Selected Poems*
selected and introduced by A.H. Ninham

The Crescent Moon Book of Love Poetry
edited by Louise Cooper

The Crescent Moon Book of Mystical Poetry in English
edited by Carol Appleby

The Crescent Moon Book of Nature Poetry From Langland to Lawrence
edited by Margaret Elvy

The Crescent Moon Book of Metaphysical Poetry
edited and introduced by Charlotte Greene

The Crescent Moon Book of Elizabethan Love Poetry
edited and introduced by Carol Appleby

The Crescent Moon Book of Romantic Poetry
edited and introduced by L.M. Poole

Peter Redgrove: Here Comes the Flood
by Jeremy Mark Robinson

Sex-Magic-Poetry-Cornwall: A Flood of Poems
by Peter Redgrove, edited with an essay by Jeremy Mark Robinson

Brigitte's Blue Heart
by Jeremy Reed

Claudia Schiffer's Red Shoes
by Jeremy Reed

By-Blows: Uncollected Poems
by D.J. Enright

Petrarch, Dante and the Troubadours: The Religion of Love and Poetry
by Cassidy Hughes

Dante: *Selections From the Vita Nuova*
translated by Thomas Okey

Arthur Rimbaud: *Selected Poems*
edited and translated by Andrew Jary

Arthur Rimbaud: *A Season in Hell*
edited and translated by Andrew Jary

Rimbaud: Arthur Rimbaud and the Magic of Poetry
by Jeremy Mark Robinson

Friedrich Hölderlin: *Hölderlin's Songs of Light: Selected Poems*
translated by Michael Hamburger

Rainer Maria Rilke: *Dance the Orange:* Selected Poems
translated by Michael Hamburger

Rilke: Space, Essence and Angels in the Poetry of Rainer Maria Rilke
by B.D. Barnacle

German Romantic Poetry: Goethe, Novalis, Heine, Hölderlin
by Carol Appleby

Arseny Tarkovsky: *Life, Life: Selected Poems*
translated by Virginia Rounding

Emily Dickinson: *Wild Nights: Selected Poems*
selected and introduced by Miriam Chalk

Cavafy: Anatomy of a Soul
by Matt Crispin

Delia

D E L I A

Samuel Daniel

Edited by Mark Tuley

CRESCENT MOON

CRESCENT MOON PUBLISHING
P.O. Box 1312, Maidstone
Kent, ME14 5XU
Great Britain
ww.crmoon.com

First published 2013.

Printed and bound in the U.S.A.
Set in Bodoni Book 11 on 13pt.
Designed by Radiance Graphics.

The right of Mark Tuley to be identified as the editor of this book
has been asserted generally in accordance with sections 77 and 78
of the Copyright, Designs and Patents Act 1988.

British Library Cataloguing in Publication data

ISBN-13 9781861712912

CONTENTS

Samuel Daniel

Samuel Daniel, by Thomas Cockson,
frontispiece for Civile War, 1609

London around 1600

Delia

TO THE LADY MARY

COUNTESS OF PEMBROKE

Wonder of these, glory of other times,
O thou whom envy ev'n is forced t'admire!
Great Patroness of these my humble rhymes,
Which thou from out thy greatness dost inspire!
Since only thou has deigned to raise them higher,
Vouchsafe now to accept them as thine own,
Begotten by thy hand and my desire,
Wherein my zeal and thy great might is shown.
And seeing this unto the world is known,
O leave not still to grace thy work in me;
Let not the quickening seed be overthrown
Of that which may be born to honor thee,
    Whereof the travail I may challenge mine,
    But yet the glory, Madam, must be thine!

TO DELIA

I

Unto the boundless ocean of thy beauty
Runs this poor river, charged with streams of zeal,
Returning thee the tribute of my duty,
Which here my love, my youth, my plaints reveal.
Here I unclasp the book of my charged soul,
Where I have cast th' accounts of all my care;
Here have I summed my sighs. Here I enrol
How they were spent for thee. Look, what they are.
Look on the dear expenses of my youth,
And see how just I reckon with thine eyes.
Examine well thy beauty with my truth,
And cross my cares ere greater sums arise.
    Read it, sweet maid, though it be done but slightly;
    Who can show all his love, doth love but lightly.

II

Go, wailing verse, the infants of my love,
Minerva-like, brought forth without a mother;
Present the image of the cares I prove,
Witness your father's grief exceeds all other.
Sigh out a story of her cruel deeds,
With interrupted accents of despair;
A monument that whosoever reads,
May justly praise and blame my loveless Fair;
Say her disdain hath dried up my blood,
And starved you, in succours still denying;
Press to her eyes, importune me some good,
Waken her sleeping pity with your crying:
     Knock at her hard heart, beg till you have moved
                                                  her,
     And tell th'unkind how dearly I have loved her.

III

If so it hap this offspring of my care,
These fatal anthems, lamentable songs,
Come to their view, who like afflicted are;
Let them yet sigh their own, and moan my wrongs.
But untouched hearts with unaffected eye,
Approach not to behold my soul's distress;
Clear-sighted you soon note what is awry,
Whilst blinded souls mine errors never guess.
You blinded souls, whom youth and error lead;
You outcast eaglets dazzled with your sun,
Do you, and none but you, my sorrows read;
You best can judge the wrongs that she hath done,
    That she hath done, the motive of my pain,
    Who whilst I love doth kill me with disdain.

IV

These plaintive verse, the posts of my desire,
Which haste for succour to her slow regard,
Bear not report of any slender fire,
Forging a grief to win a fame's reward.
Nor are my passions limned for outward hue,
For that no colours can depaint my sorrows;
Delia herself, and all the world may view
Best in my face where cares have tilled deep furrows.
No bays I seek to deck my mourning brow,
O clear-eyed rector of the holy hill!
My humble accents bear the olive bough
Of intercession but to move her will.
　　These lines I use t'unburden mine own heart;
　　My love affects no fame nor 'steems of art.

V

Whilst youth and error led my wandering mind,
And set my thoughts in heedless ways to range,
All unawares a goddess chaste I find,
Diana-like, to work my sudden change.
For her, no sooner had mine eye bewrayed,
But with disdain to see me in that place,
With fairest hand the sweet unkindest maid
Casts water-cold disdain upon my face.
Which turned my sport into a hart's despair,
Which still is chased, while I have any breath,
By mine own thoughts set on me by my Fair.
My thoughts like hounds pursue me to my death;
    Those that I fostered of mine own accord,
    Are made by her to murder thus their lord.

VI

Fair is my love, and cruel as she's fair;
Her brow shades frowns although her eyes are sunny;
Her smiles are lightning though her pride despair;
And her disdains are gall, her favours honey;
A modest maid, decked with a blush of honour,
Whose feet do tread green paths of youth and love;
The wonder of all eyes that look upon her,
Sacred on earth, designed a saint above.
Chastity and beauty, which were deadly foes,
Live reconciled friends within her brow;
And had she pity to conjoin with those,
Then who had heard the plaints I utter now?
    O had she not been fair and thus unkind,
    My Muse had slept and none had known my mind!

VII

For had she not been fair and thus unkind,
Then had no finger pointed at my lightness;
The world had never known what I do find,
And clouds obscure had shaded still her brightness.
Then had no censor's eye these lines surveyed,
Nor graver brows have judged my Muse so vain;
No sun my blush and error had bewrayed,
Nor yet the world had heard of such disdain.
Then had I walked with bold erected face;
No downcast look had signified my miss;
But my degraded hopes with such disgrace
Did force me groan out griefs and utter this.
    For being full, should I not then have spoken,
    My sense oppressed had failed and heart had
                    broken.

VIII

Thou, poor heart, sacrificed unto the fairest,
Hast sent the incense of thy sighs to heaven;
And still against her frowns fresh vows repairest,
And made thy passions with her beauty even.
And you, mine eyes, the agents of my heart,
Told the dumb message of my hidden grief;
And oft, with careful tunes, with silent art,
Did treat the cruel Fair to yield relief.
And you, my verse, the advocates of love,
Have followed hard the process of my case:
And urged that title which doth plainly prove
My faith should win, if justice might have place.
    Yet though I see that nought we do can move,
    'Tis not disdain must make me cease to love.

IX

If this be love, to draw a weary breath,
To paint on floods till the shore cry to th'air;
With downward looks still reading on the earth.
These sad memorials of my love's despair;
If this be love, to war against my soul,
Lie down to wail, rise up to sigh and grieve,
The never-resting stone of care to roll,
Still to complain my griefs, whilst none relieve;
If this be love, to clothe me with dark thoughts,
Haunting untrodden paths to wail apart,
My pleasures horror, music tragic notes,
Tears in mine eyes and sorrow at my heart;
    If this be love, to live a living death,
    Then do I love, and draw this weary breath.

X

Then do I love and draw this weary breath
For her, the cruel Fair, within whose brow
I written find the sentence of my death
In unkind letters wrote she cares not how.
Thou power that rul'st the confines of the night,
Laughter-loving goddess, worldly pleasures' queen,
Intenerate that heart that sets so light
The truest love that ever yet was seen;
And cause her leave to triumph in this wise
Upon the prostrate spoil of that poor heart
That serves, a trophy to her conquering eyes,
And must their glory to the world impart;
    Once let her know sh'hath done enough to prove
                               me,
    And let her pity if she cannot love me!

XI

Tears, vows and prayers gain the hardest hearts,
Tears, vows and prayers have I spent in vain;
Tears cannot soften flint nor vows convert;
Prayers prevail not with a quaint disdain.
I lose my tears where I have lost my love,
I vow my faith where faith is not regarded,
I pray in vain a merciless to move;
So rare a faith ought better be rewarded.
Yet though I cannot win her will with tears,
Though my soul's idol scorneth all my vows,
Though all my prayers be to so deaf ears,
No favour though the cruel Fair allows,
    Yet will I weep, vow, pray to cruel she;
    Flint, frost, disdain, wears, melts and yields, we see.

XII

My spotless love hovers with purest wings
About the temple of the proudest frame,
Where blaze those lights, fairest of earthly things;
Which clear our clouded world with brightest flame.
M'ambitious thoughts, confined in her face,
Affect no honour but what she can give;
My hopes do rest in limits of her grace;
I weigh no comfort unless she relieve.
For she that can my heart imparadise,
Holds in her fairest hand what dearest is.
My fortune's wheel's the circle of her eyes,
Whose rolling grace deign once a turn of bliss.
　　All my life's sweet consists in her alone,
　　So much I love the most unloving one.

XIII

Behold what hap Pygmalion had to frame
And carve his proper grief upon a stone!
My heavy fortune is much like the same;
I work on flint and that's the cause I moan.
For hapless lo, even with mine own desires
I figured on the table of my heart
The fairest form that the world's eye admires,
And so did perish by my proper art.
And still I toil to change the marble breast
Of her whose sweetest grace I do adore,
Yet cannot find her breathe unto my rest.
Hard is her heart, and woe is me therefore.
    O happy he that joyed his stone and art!
    Unhappy I, to love a stony heart!

XIV

Those snary locks are those same nets, my dear,
Wherewith my liberty thou didst surprise
Love was the flame that fired me so near,
The dart transpiercing were those crystal eyes.
Strong is the net, and fervent is the flame;
Deep is the wound my sighs can well report.
Yet I do love, adore, and praise the same,
That holds, that burns, that wounds in this sort;
And list not seek to break, to quench, to heal,
The bond, the flame, the wound that festereth so,
By knife, by liquor, or by salve to deal;
So much I please to perish in my woe.
     Yet lest long travails be above my strength,
     Good Delia, loose, quench, heal me, now at length!

XV

If that a loyal heart and faith unfeigned,
If a sweet languish with a chaste desire,
If hunger-starven thoughts so long retained,
Fed but with smoke, and cherished but with fire;
And if a brow with care's characters painted
Bewray my love with broken words half spoken
To her which sits in my thoughts' temple sainted,
And lays to view my vulture-gnawn heart open;
If I have done due homage to her eyes,
And had my sighs still tending on her name,
If on her love my life and honour lies,
And she, th'unkindest maid, still scorns the same;
    Let this suffice, that all the world may see
    The fault is hers, though mine the hurt must be.

XVI

Happy in sleep, waking content to languish,
Embracing clouds by night, in daytime mourn,
My joys but shadows, touch of truth my anguish,
Griefs ever springing, comforts never born;
And still expecting when she will relent,
Grown hoarse with crying, "mercy, mercy give,'
So many vows and prayers having spent
That weary of my life I loathe to live;
And yet the hydra of my cares renews
Still new-born sorrows of her fresh disdain;
And still my hope the summer winds pursues,
Finding no end nor period of my pain;
    This is my state, my griefs do touch so nearly,
    And thus I live because I love her dearly.

XVII

Why should I sing in verse? Why should I frame
These sad neglected notes for her dear sake?
Why should I offer up unto her name,
The sweetest sacrifice my youth can make?
Why should I strive to make her live for ever,
That never deigns to give me joy to live?
Why should m'afflicted Muse so much endeavour
Such honour unto cruelty to give?
If her defects have purchased her this fame,
What should her virtues do, her smiles, her love?
If this her worst, how should her best inflame?
What passions would her milder favours move?
  Favours, I think, would sense quite overcome;
  And that makes happy lovers ever dumb.

XVIII

Since the first look that led me to this error,
To this thoughts' maze to my confusion tending,
Still have I lived in grief, in hope, in terror,
The circle of my sorrows never ending;
Yet cannot leave her love that holds me hateful;
Her eyes exact it, though her heart disdains me.
See what reward he hath that serves th'ungrateful?
So true and loyal love no favour gains me.
Still must I whet my young desires abated,
Upon the flint of such a heart rebelling;
And all in vain; her pride is so innated,
She yields no place at all for pity's dwelling.
    Oft have I told her that my soul did love her,
    And that with tears; yet all this will not move her.

XIX

Restore thy tresses to the golden ore,
Yield Cytherea's son those arks of love;
Bequeath the heavens the stars that I adore,
And to the orient do thy pearls remove;
Yield thy hands' pride unto the ivory white;
T'Arabian odours give thy breathing sweet;
Restore thy blush unto Aurora bright;
To Thetis give the honour of thy feet.
Let Venus have the graces she resigned,
And thy sweet voice give back unto the spheres;
But yet restore thy fierce and cruel mind
To Hyrcan tigers and to ruthless bears;
    Yield to the marble thy hard heart again;
    So shalt thou cease to plague, and I to pain.

XX

What it is to breathe and live without life;
How to be pale with anguish, red with fear,
T'have peace abroad, and nought within but strife:
Wish to be present, and yet shun t'appear;
How to be bold far off, and bashful near;
How to think much, and have no words to speak;
To crave redress, yet hold affliction dear;
To have affection strong, a body weak,
Never to find, yet evermore to seek;
And seek that which I dare not hope to find;
T'affect this life and yet this life disleek,
Grateful t'another, to myself unkind:
    This cruel knowledge of these contraries,
    Delia, my heart hath learned out of those eyes.

XXI

If beauty thus be clouded with a frown,
That pity shines no comfort to my bliss,
And vapours of disdain so overgrown,
That my life's light wholly indarkened is,
Why should I more molest the world with cries,
The air with sighs, the earth below with tears,
Since I live hateful to those ruthful eyes,
Vexing with untuned moan her dainty ears!
If I have loved her dearer than my breath,
My breath that calls the heaven to witness it!-
And still hold her most dear until my death,
And if that all this cannot move one whit,
    Yet sure she cannot but must think apart
    She doth me wrong to grieve so true a heart.

XXII

Come Time, the anchor hold of my desire,
My last resort whereto my hopes appeal;
Cause once the date of her disdain t'exspire,
Make her the sentence of her wrath repeal.
Rob her fair brow, break in on beauty, steal
Power from those eyes which pity cannot spare;
Deal with those dainty cheeks, as she doth deal
With this poor heart consumed with despair.
This heart made now the prospective of care
By loving her, the cruelst fair that lives,
The cruelst fair that sees I pine for her,
And never mercy to thy merit gives.
    Let her not still triumph over the prize
    Of mine affections taken by her eyes.

XXIII

Time, cruel Time, come and subdue that brow
Which conquers all but thee, and thee too stays,
As if she were exempt from scythe or bow,
From love or years unsubject to decays.
Or art thou grown in league with those fair eyes,
That they may help thee to consume our days?
Or dost thou spare her for her cruelties,
Being merciless like thee that no man weighs?
And yet thou seest thy power she disobeys,
Cares not for thee, but lets thee waste in vain,
And prodigal of hours and years betrays
Beauty and youth t'opinion and disdain.
     Yet spare her, Time; let her exempted be;
     She may become more kind to thee or me.

XXIV

These sorrowing sighs, the smoke of mine annoy,
These tears, which heat of sacred flame distils,
Are those due tributes that my faith doth pay
Unto the tyrant whose unkindness kills.
I sacrifice my youth and blooming years
At her proud feet, and she respects not it;
My flower, untimely's withered with my tears,
By winter woes for spring of youth unfit.
She thinks a look may recompense my care,
And so with looks prolongs my long-looked ease;
As short that bliss, so is the comfort rare;
Yet must that bliss my hungry thoughts appease.
      Thus she returns my hopes so fruitless ever;
      Once let her love indeed, or eye me never!

XXV

False hope prolongs my ever certain grief,
Traitor to me, and faithful to my love.
A thousand times it promised me relief,
Yet never any true effect I prove.
Oft when I find in her no truth at all,
I banish her, and blame her treachery;
Yet soon again I must her back recall,
As one that dies without her company.
Thus often, as I chase my hope from me,
Straightway she hastes her unto Delia's eyes;
Fed with some pleasing look, there shall she be,
And so sent back. And thus my fortune lies;
    Looks feed my hope, hope fosters me in vain;
    Hopes are unsure when certain is my pain.

XXVI

Look in my griefs, and blame me not to mourn,
From care to care that leads a life so bad;
Th'orphan of fortune, born to be her scorn,
Whose clouded brow doth make my days so sad.
Long are their nights whose cares do never sleep,
Loathsome their days who never sun yet joyed;
The impression of her eyes do pierce so deep,
That thus I live both day and night annoyed.
Yet since the sweetest root yields fruit so sour,
Her praise from my complaint I may not part;
I love th'effect, the cause being of this power;
I'll praise her face and blame her flinty heart,
   Whilst we both make the world admire at us,
   Her for disdain, and me for loving thus.

XXVII

Reignin my thoughts, fair hand, sweet eye, rare voice!
Possess me whole, my heart's triumvirate!
Yet heavy heart, to make so hard a choice
Of such as spoil thy poor afflicted state!
For whilst they strive which shall be lord of all,
All my poor life by them is trodden down;
They all erect their trophies on my fall,
And yield me nought that gives them their renown.
When back I look, I sigh my freedom past,
And wail the state wherein I present stand,
And see my fortune ever like to last,
Finding me reined with such a heavy hand.
 What can I do but yield? and yield I do;
  And serve all three, and yet they spoil me too!

XXVIII

*Alluding to the sparrow pursued by a hawk, that flew
into the bosom of Zenocrates*

Whilst by thy eyes pursued, my poor heart flew
Into the sacred refuge of thy breast;
Thy rigour in that sanctuary slew
That which thy succ'ring mercy should have blest.
No privilege of faith could it protect,
Faith being with blood and five years witness signed,
Wherein no show gave cause of least suspect,
For well thou saw'st my love and how I pined.
Yet no mild comfort would thy brow reveal,
No lightning looks which falling hopes erect;
What boots to laws of succour to appeal?
Ladies and tyrants never laws respect.
    Then there I die from whence my life should come,
    And by that hand whom such deeds ill become.

XXIX

Still in the trace of one perplexed thought,
My ceaseless cares continually run on,
Seeking in vain what I have ever sought,
One in my love, and her hard heart still one.
I who did never joy in other sun,
And have no stars but those that must fulfil
The work of rigour, fatally begun
Upon this heart whom cruelty will kill,
Injurious Delia!-yet, I love thee still,
And will whilst I shall draw this breath of mine;
I'll tell the world that I deserved but ill,
And blame myself, t'excuse that heart of thine;
 See then who sins the greater of us twain,
 I in my love, or thou in thy disdain.

XXX

Oft do I marvel whether Delia's eyes
Are eyes, or else two radiant stars that shine;
For how could nature ever thus devise
Of earth, on earth, a substance so divine?
Stars, sure, they are, whose motions rule desires,
And calm and tempest follow their aspects;
Their sweet appearing still such power inspires,
That makes the world admire so strange effects.
Yet whether fixed or wandering stars are they,
Whose influence rules the orb of my poor heart;
Fixed, sure, they are, but wandering make me stray
In endless errors whence I cannot part.
    Stars, then, not eyes, move you with milder view
    Your sweet aspect on him that honours you!

XXXI

The star of my mishap imposed this pain
To spend the April of my years in grief;
Finding my fortune ever in the wane,
With still fresh cares, supplied with no relief.
Yet thee I blame not, though for thee 'tis done;
But these weak wings presuming to aspire,
Which now are melted by thine eyes' bright sun
That makes me fall from off my high desire;
And in my fall I cry for help with speed,
No pitying eye looks back upon my fears;
No succour find I now when most I need:
My heats must drown in th'ocean of my tears,
    Which still must bear the title of my wrong,
    Caused by those cruel beams that were so strong.

XXXII

And yet I cannot reprehend the flight,
Or blame th'attempt, presuming so to soar;
The mounting venture for a high delight
Did make the honour of the fall the more.
For who gets wealth, that puts not from the shore?
Danger hath honours, great designs their fame,
Glory doth follow, courage goes before;
And though th'event oft answers not the same,
Suffice that high attempts have never shame.
The mean observer whom base safety keeps,
Lives without honour, dies without a name,
And in eternal darkness ever sleeps.
    And therefore, Delia, 'tis to me no blot
    To have attempted though attained thee not.

XXXIII

Raising my hopes on hills of high desire,
Thinking to scale the heaven of her heart,
My slender means presumed too high a part,
Her thunder of disdain forced me retire,
And threw me down to pain in all this fire,
Where lo, I languish in so heavy smart
Because th'attempt was far above my art;
Her pride brooked not poor souls should come so nigh
                                                    her.
Yet, I protest, my high desiring will
Was not to dispossess her of her right;
Her sovereignty should have remained still;
I only sought the bliss to have her sight.
        Her sight, contented thus to see me spill,
        Framed my desires fit for her eyes to kill.

XXXIV

Why dost thou, Delia, credit so thy glass,
Gazing thy beauty deigned thee by the skies,
And dost not rather look on him, alas!
Whose state best shows the force of murdering eyes?
The broken tops of lofty trees declare
The fury of a mercy-wanting storm;
And of what force thy wounding graces are
Upon myself, you best may find the form.
Then leave thy glass, and gaze thyself on me;
That mirror shows what power is in thy face;
To view your form too much may danger be,
Narcissus changed t'a flower in such a case.
     And you are changed, but not t'a hyacinth;
        I fear your eye hath turned your heart to flint.

XXXV

I once may see when years shall wreck my wrong,
And golden hairs shall change to silver wire,
And those bright rays that kindle all this fire,
Shall fail in force, their working not so strong,
Then beauty, now the burden of my song,
Whose glorious blaze the world doth so admire,
Must yield up all to tyrant Time's desire;
Then fade those flowers that decked her pride so long.
When if she grieve to gaze her in her glass,
Which then presents her whiter-withered hue,
Go you, my verse, go tell her what she was,
For what she was, she best shall find in you.
    Your fiery heat lets not her glory pass,
    But phoenix-like shall make her live anew.

XXXVI

Look, Delia, how w'esteem the half-blown rose,
The image of thy blush, and summer's honour,
Whilst yet her tender bud doth undisclose
That full of beauty time bestows upon her.
No sooner spreads her glory in the air,
But straight her wide-blown pomp comes to decline;
She then is scorned that late adorned the fair;
So fade the roses of those cheeks of thine.
No April can revive thy withered flowers,
Whose springing grace adorns thy glory now;
Swift speedy time, feathered with flying hours,
Dissolves the beauty of the fairest brow.
     Then do not thou such treasure waste in vain,
     But love now whilst thou mayst be loved again.

XXXVII

But love whilst that thou mayst be loved again,
Now whilst thy May hath filled thy lap with flowers,
Now whilst thy beauty bears without a stain,
Now use thy summer smiles, ere winter lowers.
And whilst thou spread'st unto the rising sun,
The fairest flower that ever saw the light,
Now joy thy time before thy sweet be done;
And, Delia, think thy morning must have night,
And that thy brightness sets at length to west,
When thou wilt close up that which now thou showest,
And think the same becomes thy fading best,
Which then shall most inveil and shadow most.
    Men do not weigh the stalk for that it was,
    When once they find her flower, her glory pass.

XXXVIII

When men shall find thy flower, thy glory pass,
And thou with careful brow sitting alone
Received hast this message from thy glass
That tells the truth, and says that all is gone;
Fresh shalt thou see in me the wounds thou mad'st,
Though spent thy flame, in me the heat remaining.
I that have loved thee thus before thou fad'st,
My faith shall wax when thou art in thy waning.
The world shall find this miracle in me,
That fire can burn when all the matter's spent;
Then what my faith hath been thyself shalt see,
And that thou wast unkind thou mayst repent.
    Thou mayst repent that thou hast scorned my tears,
    When winter snows upon thy sable hairs.

XXXIX

When winter snows upon thy sable hairs,
And frost of age hath nipped thy beauties near,
When dark shall seem thy day that never clears,
And all lies withered that was held so dear;
Then take this picture which I here present thee,
Limned with a pencil not all unworthy;
Here see the gifts that God and nature lent thee,
Here read thyself and what I suffered for thee.
This may remain thy lasting monument,
Which happily posterity may cherish;
These colours with thy fading are not spent,
These may remain when thou and I shall perish.
    If they remain, then thou shalt live thereby;
    They will remain, and so thou canst not die.

XL

Thou canst not die whilst any zeal abound
In feeling hearts than can conceive these lines;
Though thou a Laura hast no Petrarch found,
In base attire yet clearly beauty shines.
And I though born within a colder clime,
Do feel mine inward heat as great-I know it;
He never had more faith, although more rhyme;
I love as well though he could better show it.
But I may add one feather to thy fame,
To help her flight throughout the fairest isle;
And if my pen could more enlarge thy name,
Then shouldst thou live in an immortal style.
    For though that Laura better limned be,
    Suffice, thou shalt be loved as well as she!

XLI

Be not displeased that these my papers should
Bewray unto the world how fair thou art;
Or that my wits have showed the best they could
The chastest flame that ever warmed heart.
Think not, sweet Delia, this shall be thy shame,
My muse should sound thy praise with mournful warble.
How many live, the glory of whose name
Shall rest in ice, while thine is graved in marble!
Thou mayst in after ages live esteemed,
Unburied in these lines, reserved in pureness;
These shall entomb those eyes, that have redeemed
Me from the vulgar, thee from all obscureness.
　　Although my careful accents never moved thee,
　　Yet count it no disgrace that I loved thee.

XLII

Delia, these eyes that so admireth thine,
Have seen those walls which proud ambition reared
To check the world, how they entombed have lain
Within themselves, and on them ploughs have eared;
Yet never found that barbarous hand attained
The spoil of fame deserved by virtuous men,
Whose glorious actions luckily had gained
Th'eternal annals of a happy pen.
And therefore grieve not if thy beauties die
Though time do spoil thee of the fairest veil
That ever yet covered mortality,
And must instar the needle and the rail.
    That grace which doth more than inwoman thee,
    Lives in my lines and must eternal be.

XLIII

Most fair and lovely maid, look from the shore,
See thy Leander striving in these waves,
Poor soul quite spent, whose force can do no more.
Now send forth hope, for now calm pity saves,
And waft him to thee with those lovely eyes,
A happy convoy to a holy land.
Now show thy power, and where thy virtue lies;
To save thine own, stretch out the fairest hand.
Stretch out the fairest hand, a pledge of peace,
That hand that darts so right and never misses;
I shall forget old wrongs, my griefs shall cease;
And that which gave me wounds, I'll give it kisses.
　　Once let the ocean of my care find shore,
　　That thou be pleased, and I may sigh no more.

XLIV

Read in my face a volume of despairs,
The wailing Iliads of my tragic woe;
Drawn with my blood, and painted with my cares,
Wrought by her hand that I have honoured so.
Who whilst I burn, she sings at my soul's wrack,
Looking aloft from turret of her pride;
There my soul's tyrant joys her in the sack
Of her own seat, whereof I made her guide.
There do these smokes that from affliction rise,
Serve as an incense to a cruel dame;
A sacrifice thrice-grateful to her eyes,
Because their power serves to exact the same.
    Thus ruins she to satisfy her will,
    The temple where her name was honoured still.

XLV

My Delia hath the waters of mine eyes,
The ready handmaids on her grace t'attend,
That never fail to ebb, but ever rise;
For to their flow she never grants an end.
The ocean never did attend more duly
Upon his sovereign's course, the night's pale queen,
Nor paid the impost of his waves more truly,
Than mine unto her cruelty hath been.
Yet nought the rock of that hard heart can move,
Where beat these tears with zeal, and fury drives;
And yet, I'd rather languish in her love,
Than I would joy the fairest she that lives.
    And if I find such pleasure to complain,
    What should I do then if I should obtain?

XLVI

How long shall I in mine affliction mourn,
A burden to myself, distressed in mind;
When shall my interdicted hopes return
From out despair wherein they live confined?
When shall her troubled brow charged with disdain
Reveal the treasure which her smiles impart?
When shall my faith the happiness attain,
To break the ice that hath congealed her heart?
Unto herself, herself my love doth summon,
(If love in her hath any power to move)
And let her tell me, as she is a woman,
Whether my faith hath not deserved her love?
    I know her heart cannot but judge with me,
    Although her eyes my adversaries be.

XLVII

Beauty, sweet love, is like the morning dew,
Whose short refresh upon the tender green
Cheers for a time but till the sun doth show,
And straight 'tis gone as it had never been.
Soon doth it fade that makes the fairest flourish,
Short is the glory of the blushing rose,
The hue which thou so carefully dost nourish,
Yet which at length thou must be forced to lose.
When thou, surcharged with burden of thy years,
Shalt bend thy wrinkles homeward to the earth,
And that in beauty's lease expired appears
The date of age, the kalends of our death,-
  But ah! no more, this must not be foretold,
  For women grieve to think they must be old.

XLVIII

I must not grieve my love, whose eyes would read
Lines of delight, whereon her youth might smile;
Flowers have a time before they come to seed,
And she is young, and now must sport the while.
Ah sport, sweet maid, in season of these years,
And learn to gather flowers before they wither.
And where the sweetest blossoms first appears,
Let love and youth conduct thy pleasures thither.
Lighten forth smiles to clear the clouded air,
And calm the tempest which my sighs do raise;
Pity and smiles do best become the fair,
Pity and smiles shall yield thee lasting praise.
    Make me to say, when all my griefs are gone,
    Happy the heart that sighed for such a one!

XLIX

At the Author's going into Italy

Ah whither, poor forsaken, wilt thou go,
To go from sorrow and thine own distress,
When every place presents like face of woe,
And no remove can make thy sorrows less!
Yet go, forsaken! Leave these woods, these plains,
Leave her and all, and all for her that leaves
Thee and thy love forlorn, and both disdains,
And of both wrongful deems and ill conceives.
Seek out some place, and see if any place
Can give the least release unto thy grief;
Convey thee from the thought of thy disgrace,
Steal from thyself and be thy cares' own thief.
    But yet what comforts shall I hereby gain?
    Bearing the wound, I needs must feel the pain.

L

This Sonnet was made at the Author's being in Italy

Drawn with th'attractive virtue of her eyes,
My touched heart turns it to that happy coast,
My joyful north, where all my fortune lies,
The level of my hopes desired most;
There where my Delia, fairer than the sun,
Decked with her youth whereon the world doth smile,
Joys in that honour which her eyes have won,
Th'eternal wonder of our happy isle.
Flourish, fair Albion, glory of the north!
Neptune's best darling, held between his arms;
Divided from the world as better worth,
Kept for himself, defended from all harms!
    Still let disarmed peace deck her and thee;
    And Muse-foe Mars abroad far fostered be!

LI

Care-charmer sleep, son of the sable night,
Brother to death, in silent darkness born,
Relieve my languish, and restore the light;
With dark forgetting of my care return,
And let the day be time enough to mourn
The shipwreck of my ill-adventured youth;
Let waking eyes suffice to wail their scorn,
Without the torment of the night's untruth.
Cease, dreams, the images of day-desires,
To model forth the passions of the morrow;
Never let rising sun approve you liars,
To add more grief to aggravate my sorrow;
    Still let me sleep, embracing clouds in vain,
    And never wake to feel the day's disdain.

LII

Let others sing of knights and paladins,
In aged accents and untimely words,
Paint shadows in imaginary lines
Which well the reach of their high wits records;
But I must sing of thee and those fair eyes
Authentic shall my verse in time to come,
When yet th'unborn shall say, Lo, where she lies,
Whose beauty made him speak that else was dumb!
These are the arks, the trophies I erect,
That fortify thy name against old age;
And these thy sacred virtues must protect
Against the dark and time's consuming rage.
    Though th'error of my youth in them appear,
    Suffice, they show I lived and loved thee, dear.

LIII

As to the Roman that would free his land,
His error was his honour and renown;
And more the fame of his mistaking hand
Than if he had the tyrant overthrown.
So Delia, hath mine error made me known,
And my deceived attempt deserved more fame,
Than if had the victory mine own,
And thy hard heart had yielded up the same.
And so likewise renowned is thy blame;
Thy cruelty, thy glory; O strange case,
That errors should be graced that merit shame,
And sin of frowns bring honour to the face.
  Yet happy Delia that thou wast unkind,
   Though happier far, if thou would'st change thy
              mind.

LIV

Like as the lute delights or else dislikes
As is his art that plays upon the same,
So sounds my Muse according as she strikes
On my heart-strings high tuned unto her fame.
Her touch doth cause the warble of the sound,
Which here I yield in lamentable wise,
A wailing descant on the sweetest ground,
Whose due reports give honour to her eyes;
Else harsh my style, untunable my Muse;
Hoarse sounds the voice that praiseth not her name;
If any pleasing relish here I use,
Then judge the world her beauty gives the same.
    For no ground else could make the music such,
    Nor other hand could give so sweet a touch.

LV

None other fame mine unambitious Muse
Affected ever but t'eternise thee;
All other honours do my hopes refuse,
Which meaner prized and momentary be.
For God forbid I should my papers blot
With mercenary lines with servile pen,
Praising virtues in them that have them not,
Basely attending on the hopes of men.
No, no, my verse respects not Thames, nor theatres;
Nor seeks it to be known unto the great;
But Avon, poor in fame, and poor in waters,
Shall have my song, where Delia hath her seat.
    Avon shall be my Thames, and she my song;
    No other prouder brooks shall hear my wrong.

LVI

Unhappy pen, and ill-accepted lines
That intimate in vain my chaste desire,
My chaste desire, which from dark sorrow shines,
Enkindled by her eyes' celestial fire;
Celestial fire, and unrespecting powers
Which pity not the wounds made by their might,
Showed in these lines, the work of careful hours,
The sacrifice here offered to her sight.
But since she weighs them not, this rests for me:
I'll moan myself, and hide the wrong I have,
And so content me that her frowns should be
To m'infant style the cradle and the grave.
    What though my Muse no honour get thereby;
    Each bird sings to herself, and so will I.

LVII

Lo here the impost of a faith entire,
That love doth pay, and her disdain extorts;
Behold the message of a chaste desire
That tells the world how much my grief imports.
These tributary passions, beauty's due,
I send those eyes, the cabinets of love;
That cruelty herself might grieve to view
Th'affliction her unkind disdain doth move.
And how I live, cast down from off all mirth,
Pensive, alone, only but with despair;
My joys abortive perish in their birth,
My griefs long-lived and care succeeding care.
    This is my state, and Delia's heart is such;
    I say no more, I fear I said too much.

REJECTED SONNETS

Included below are some of the sonnets rejected from later editions of *Delia*. They were printed in the 1591 edition of Newman.

I

The only bird alone that nature frames,
When weary of the tedious life she lives,
By fire dies, yet finds new life in flames,
Her ashes to her shape new essence gives.
When only I, the only wretched wight,
Weary of life that breathes but sorrow's blast,
Pursue the flame of such a beauty bright,
That burns my heart, and yet my life still lasts.
O sovereign light, that with thy sacred flame
Consumes my life, revive me after this!
And make me, with the happy bird, the same
That dies to live, by favour of thy bliss!
    This deed of thine will show a goddess' power,
    In so long death to grant one living hour.

II

The sly enchanter when to work his will
And secret wrong on some forespoken wight,
Frames wax in form to represent aright
The poor unwitting wretch he means to kill,
And pricks the image framed by magic's skill,
Whereby to vex the party day and night;
Like hath she done, whose show bewitched my sight
To beauty's charms, her lover's blood to spill.
For first, like wax she framed me by her eyes,
Whose rays sharp-pointed set upon my breast
Martyr my life and plague me in this wise
With ling'ring pain to perish in unrest.
  Nought could, save this, my sweetest fair suffice,
  To try her art on him that loves her best.

III

The tablet of my heavy fortunes here
Upon thine altar, Paphian Power, I place.
The grievous shipwreck of my travels dear
In bulged bark, all perished in disgrace.
That traitor Love was pilot to my woe;
My sails were hope, spread with my sighs of grief;
The twin lights which my hapless course did show
Hard by th'inconstant sands of false relief,
Were two bright stars which led my view apart.
A siren's voice allured me come so near
To perish on the marble of her heart,
A danger which my soul did never fear.
    Lo, thus he fares that trusts a calm too much;
    And thus fare I whose credit hath been such!

IV

Weigh but the cause, and give me leave to plain me,
For all my hurt, that my heart's queen hath wrought it;
She whom I love so dear, the more to pain me,
Withholds my right where I have dearly bought it.
Dearly I bought that was so slightly rated,
Even with the price of blood and body's wasting;
She would not yield that ought might be abated,
For all she saw my love was pure and lasting,
And yet now scorns performance of the passion,
And with her presence justice overruleth.
She tells me flat her beauty bears no action;
And so my plea and process she excludeth.
    What wrong she doth, the world may well perceive
                                    it,
    To accept my faith at first, and then to leave it.

V

Oft and in vain my rebel thoughts have ventured
To stop the passage of my vanquished heart;
And shut those ways my friendly foe first entered,
Hoping thereby to free my better part.
And whilst I guard the windows of this fort,
Where my heart's thief to vex me made her choice,
And thither all my forces do transport,
Another passage opens at her voice.
Her voice betrays me to her hand and eye,
My freedom's tyrant, conquering all by art;
But ah! what glory can she get thereby,
With three such powers to plague one silly heart!
    Yet my soul's sovereign, since I must resign,
    Reign in my thoughts, my love and life are thine!

VI[1]

Like as the spotless ermelin distressed
Circumpassed round with filth and lothsome mud,
Pines in her grief, imprisoned to her nest,
And cannot issue forth to seek her good;
So I invironed with a hatefull want,
Look to the heavens; the heavens yield forth no grace;
I search the earth, the earth I find as scant,
I view myself, myself in wofull case.
Heaven nor earth will not, myself cannot make
A way through want to free my soul from care;
But I must pine, and in my pining lurk
Lest my sad looks bewray me how I fare.
    My fortune mantled with a cloud s'obscure,
    Thus shades my life so long as wants endure.

---

1 These last two sonnets were including in the edition of *Delia* printed in 1592, but were dropped from later editions.

VII

My cares draw on mine everlasting night,
In horror's sable clouds sets my life's sun;
My life's sweet sun, my dearest comfort's light
Shall rise no more to me whose day is done.
I'll go before unto the myrtle shades,
T'attend the presence of my world's dear;
And there prepare her flowers that never fades,
And all things fit against her coming there.
If any ask me why so soon I came,
I'll hide her sin and say it was my lot.
In life and death I'll tender her good name;
My life nor death shall never be her blot.
    Although this world may seem her deed to blame,
    The Elysian ghosts shall never know the same.

A NOTE ON SAMUEL DANIEL

Samuel Daniel was born in 1562 in Taunton, Somerset. He was educated at Oxford (Magdalen Hall); he worked as a tutor (to William Herbert), and a court official. His patrons included Fulke Greville and the Earl of Devonshire. He wrote plays as well as poetry (his 1605 *Philotas* tragedy was deemed anti-royal, and sympathetic to the Earl of Essex's rebellion). He died in 1619.

Samuel Daniel's *Delia* was first published in a pirated edition in 1591 (alongside Sir Philip Sidney's *Astrophel and Stella*). In 1592, Daniel published his own edition of *Delia: Contayning Certayne Sonnets: With the Complaint of Rosamond* (50 poems). *Delia* was reprinted and revised in 1592 (again), 1594, 1595, 1598, 1601, 1602, 1622 and 1632.

Delia (another name for the goddess Diana) may have been addressed to Sir Philip Sidney's sister, the Countess of Pembroke (she is one of the recurring figures in Elizabethan sonneteering, and *Delia* was dedicated to her). Someone who lived in Beckington, Wiltshire (close to where Samuel Daniel lived), has also been suggested.

FURTHER READING

SAMUEL DANIEL

The Complete Works In Verse and Prose, ed. Grossart, 1885/ 1963
Samuel Daniel, J. Rees, Liverpool, 1964
Poems and a Defence of Ryme, ed. A.C. Sprague, London, 1930/
50/ 71

HIGHLY RECOMMENDED

The following books are excellent introductions to the
Elizabethan sonnet. Maurice Evans' *Elizabethan Sonnets* (1977,
later revised, in 1994) is one of the best books as an all-round
collection of Elizabethan sonneteering.

Maurice Evans, ed. *Elizabethan Sonnets*, Dent, 1977/ 94
G. Hiller, ed. *Poems of the Elizabethan Age*, Methuen, 1977
E. Lucie-Smith, ed. *The Penguin Book of Elizabethan Verse*,
Penguin, 1965
Michael R.G. Spiller. *The Development of the Sonnet: An Intro-
duction*, Routledge, 1992
Maurice Valency. *In Praise of Love: An Introduction to the Love-
Poetry of the Renaissance*, Macmillan, New York, 1961

OTHER BOOKS

Books marked with an asterisk are especially useful.

Sandra Berman. *The Sonnet Over Time*, Chapel Hill, 1988 •
Harold Bloom, ed. *Shakespeare's Sonnets* Chelsea House, New
    York, 1987
—. *Hamlet*, Chelsea House, New York, 1990
S. Booth. *An Essay on Shakespeare's Sonnets* Yale University
    Press, 1969
S.C. Campbell. *Only Begotten Sonnets: A Reconstruction of Shake-
    speare's Sonnets Sequence* Bell & Hyman, 1978
Reed Way Dasenbrock. *Imitating the Italians: Wyatt, Spenser,
    Syne, Pound, Joyce,* John Hopkins University Press, Baltimore,
    1991
Heather Dubrow. *Captive Victors: Shakespeare's Narrative Poems
    and Sonnets,* Cornell University Press, Ithaca, 1987
—. *Echoes of Desire: English Petrarchism and Its Counter-
    discourses,* Cornell University Press, 1995 *
Joel Fineman. *Shakespeare's Perjured Eye: The Invention of Poetic
    Subjectivity in the Sonnets* University of California Press, 1988*
Edward Hubler. *The Sense of Shakespeare's Sonnets* Hill & Wang,
    New York, 1962
J.B. Leishman. *Themes and Variations in Shakespeare's Sonnets*
    Hillary House, New York, 1963
J. W. Lever. *The Elizabethan Love Sonnet* Methuen, 1956
Arthur Marotti. ""Love is not love": Elizabethan Sonnet Sequences
    and the Social Order", *English Literary History,* 49, 1982
Kenneth Muir. *Shakespeare's Sonnets* Allen & Unwin, 1979
G.M. Ridden. *Shakespeare's Sonnets* Longman, 1982
Brent Stirling. *The Shakespeare Sonnet Order: Poems and Groups*
    University of California Press, Berkeley, 1968
J.C. Wait. *The Background to Shakespeare's Sonnets* Chatto &
    Windus, 1972
James Winny. *The Master-Mistress: A Study of Shakespeare's
    Sonnets*, Chatto & Windus, 1968

ARTS, PAINTING, SCULPTURE

The Art of Andy Goldsworthy
Andy Goldsworthy: Touching Nature
Andy Goldsworthy in Close-Up
Andy Goldsworthy: Pocket Guide
Andy Goldsworthy In America
Land Art: A Complete Guide
The Art of Richard Long
Richard Long: Pocket Guide
Land Art In Great Britain
Land Art in Close-Up
Land Art In the U.S.A.
Land Art: Pocket Guide
Installation Art in Close-Up
Minimal Art and Artists In the 1960s and After
Colourfield Painting
Land Art DVD, TV documentary
Andy Goldsworthy DVD, TV documentary
The Erotic Object: Sexuality in Sculpture From Prehistory to the Present Day
Sex in Art: Pornography and Pleasure in Painting and Sculpture
Postwar Art
Sacred Gardens: The Garden in Myth, Religion and Art
Glorification: Religious Abstraction in Renaissance and 20th Century Art
Early Netherlandish Painting
Jasper Johns
Brice MardenLeonardo da Vinci
Piero della Francesca
Giovanni Bellini
Fra Angelico: Art and Religion in the Renaissance
Mark Rothko: The Art of Transcendence
Frank Stella: American Abstract Artist
Alison Wilding: The Embrace of Sculpture
Vincent van Gogh: Visionary Landscapes
Eric Gill: Nuptials of God
Constantin Brancusi: Sculpting the Essence of Things
Max Beckmann
Gustave Moreau
Caravaggio
Egon Schiele: Sex and Death In Purple Stockings
Delizioso Fotografico Fervore: Works In Process 1
Sacro Cuore: Works In Process 2
The Light Eternal: J.M.W. Turner
The Madonna Glorified: Karen Arthurs

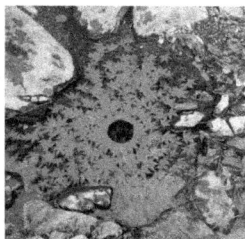

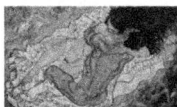

LITERATURE

J.R.R. Tolkien: The Books, The Films, The Whole Cultural Phenomenon
J.R.R. Tolkien: Pocket Guide
Beauties, Beasts and Enchantment: Classic French Fairy Tales
Tolkien's Heroic Quest
Brothers Grimm: German Popular Stories
Sexing Hardy: Thomas Hardy and Feminism
Thomas Hardy's *Tess of the d'Urbervilles*
Thomas Hardy's *Jude the Obscure*
Thomas Hardy: The Tragic Novels
Love and Tragedy: Thomas Hardy
The Poetry of Landscape in Hardy
Wessex Revisited: Thomas Hardy and John Cowper Powys
Wolfgang Iser: Essays and Interviews
Petrarch, Dante and the Troubadours
Maurice Sendak and the Art of Children's Book Illustration
Andrea Dworkin
Cixous, Irigaray, Kristeva: The *Jouissance* of French Feminism
Julia Kristeva: Art, Love, Melancholy, Philosophy, Semiotics and Psychoanalysis
Hélene Cixous I Love You: The *Jouissance* of Writing
Luce Irigaray: Lips, Kissing, and the Politics of Sexual Difference
Peter Redgrove: Here Comes the Flood
Peter Redgrove: Sex-Magic-Poetry-Cornwall
Lawrence Durrell: Between Love and Death, East and West
Love, Culture & Poetry: Lawrence Durrell
Cavafy: Anatomy of a Soul
German Romantic Poetry: Goethe, Novalis, Heine, Hölderlin
Novalis: *Hymns To the Night*
Feminism and Shakespeare
Shakespeare: *The Sonnets*
Shakespeare: Love, Poetry & Magic
The Passion of D.H. Lawrence
D.H. Lawrence: Symbolic Landscapes
D.H. Lawrence: Infinite Sensual Violence
The Ecstasies of John Cowper Powys
Sensualism and Mythology: The Wessex Novels of John Cowper Powys
Amorous Life: John Cowper Powys (H.W. Fawkner)
Postmodern Powys: New Essays on John Cowper Powys (Joe Boulter)
Rethinking Powys: Critical Essays on John Cowper Powys
Paul Bowles & Bernardo Bertolucci
Rainer Maria Rilke
Joseph Conrad: *Heart of Darkness*
In the Dim Void: Samuel Beckett
Samuel Beckett Goes into the Silence
André Gide: Fiction and Fervour
Jackie Collins and the Blockbuster Novel
Blinded By Her Light: The Love-Poetry of Robert Graves

POETRY

Ursula Le Guin: *Walking In Cornwall*
Peter Redgrove: Here Comes The Flood
Peter Redgrove: Sex-Magic-Poetry-Cornwall
Dante: Selections From the *Vita Nuova*
Petrarch, Dante and the Troubadours
William Shakespeare: *The Sonnets*
William Shakespeare: Complete Poems
Blinded By Her Light: The Love-Poetry of Robert Graves
Emily Dickinson: Selected Poems
Emily Brontë: Poems
Thomas Hardy: Selected Poems
Percy Bysshe Shelley: Poems
John Keats: Selected Poems
John Keats: Poems of 1820
D.H. Lawrence: Selected Poems
Edmund Spenser: Poems
Edmund Spenser: *Amoretti*
John Donne: Poems
Henry Vaughan: Poems
Sir Thomas Wyatt: Poems
Robert Herrick: Selected Poems
Rilke: Space, Essence and Angels in the Poetry of Rainer Maria Rilke
Rainer Maria Rilke: Selected Poems
Friedrich Hölderlin: Selected Poems
Arseny Tarkovsky: Selected Poems
Paul Verlaine: Selected Poems
Novalis: *Hymns To the Night*
Arthur Rimbaud: Selected Poems
Arthur Rimbaud: *A Season in Hell*
Arthur Rimbaud and the Magic of Poetry
D.J. Enright: By-Blows
Jeremy Reed: *Brigitte's Blue Heart*
Jeremy Reed: *Claudia Schiffer's Red Shoes*
Gorgeous Little Orpheus
Radiance: New Poems
Crescent Moon Book of Nature Poetry
Crescent Moon Book of Love Poetry
Crescent Moon Book of Mystical Poetry
Crescent Moon Book of Elizabethan Love Poetry
Crescent Moon Book of Metaphysical Poetry
Crescent Moon Book of Romantic Poetry
Pagan America: New American Poetry

MEDIA, CINEMA, FEMINISM and CULTURAL STUDIES

J.R.R. Tolkien: The Books, The Films, The Whole Cultural Phenomenon
J.R.R. Tolkien: Pocket Guide
The *Lord of the Rings* Movies: Pocket Guide
The Ghost Dance: The Origins of Religion
The Cinema of Hayao Miyazaki
Hayao Miyazaki: *Princess Mononoke*: Pocket Movie Guide
Hayao Miyazaki: *Spirited Away*: Pocket Movie Guide
The Peyote Cult
Cixous, Irigaray, Kristeva: The *Jouissance* of French Feminism
Julia Kristeva: Art, Love, Melancholy, Philosophy, Semiotics and Psychoanalysis
Luce Irigaray: Lips, Kissing, and the Politics of Sexual Difference
Hélene Cixous I Love You: The *Jouissance* of Writing
Andrea Dworkin
'Cosmo Woman': The World of Women's Magazines
Women in Pop Music
Discovering the Goddess (Geoffrey Ashe)
The Poetry of Cinema
The Sacred Cinema of Andrei Tarkovsky
Andrei Tarkovsky: Pocket Guide
Andrei Tarkovsky: *Mirror*: Pocket Movie Guide
Walerian Borowczyk: Cinema of Erotic Dreams
Jean-Luc Godard: The Passion of Cinema
Jean-Luc Godard: Pocket Guide
John Hughes and Eighties Cinema
Ferris Buller's Day Off: Pocket Movie Guide
The Cinema of Richard Linklater
Liv Tyler: Star In Ascendance
Blade Runner and the Films of Philip K. Dick
Paul Bowles and Bernardo Bertolucci
Media Hell: Radio, TV and the Press
Detonation Britain: Nuclear War in the UK
Feminism and Shakespeare
Wild Zones: Pornography, Art and Feminism
Sex in Art: Pornography and Pleasure in Painting and Sculpture
Sexing Hardy: Thomas Hardy and Feminism

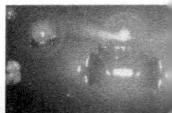

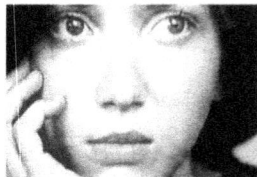

The Light Eternal is a model monograph, an exemplary job. The subject matter of the book beautifully organised and dead on beam. (Lawrence Durrell)

It is amazing for me to see my work treated with such passion and respect. (Andrea Dworkin)

Sex-Magic-Poetry-Cornwall is a very rich essay... It is like a brightly-lighted box. (Peter Redgrove)

CRESCENT MOON PUBLISHING P.O. Box 1312, Maidstone, Kent, ME14 5XU, England
0044-1622-729593   cresmopub@yahoo.co.uk   www.crmoon.com

www.ingramcontent.com/pod-product-compliance
Lightning Source LLC
Chambersburg PA
CBHW051736040426
42447CB00008B/1154